SUTTER'S MILL

AND THE CALIFORNIA
GOLD RUSH:
SEPARATING FACT FROM FICTION

by Carol Kim

CAPSTONE PRESS
a capstone imprint

Published by Capstone Press, an imprint of Capstone.
1710 Roe Crest Drive, North Mankato, Minnesota 56003
capstonepub.com

Library of Congress Cataloging-in-Publication Data
Names: Kim, Carol, author.
Title: Sutter's Mill and the California gold rush : separating fact from fiction / Carol Kim.
Description: [North Mankato] : Capstone Press, [2023] | Series: Fact vs. fiction in U.S. history | Includes bibliographical references and index. | Audience: Ages 8-11 | Audience: Grades 4-6 | Summary: "In 1848, gold was discovered at Sutter's Mill in Coloma, California. Word quickly spread, and the California Gold Rush was on! Thousands of people went to California in hopes of finding gold and striking it rich. But did that really happen? What was the real impact of so many miners rushing to the state? Discover what's real and what's fiction about the California Gold Rush through infographics, primary sources, and expertly leveled text"— Provided by publisher.
Identifiers: LCCN 2022029326 (print) | LCCN 2022029327 (ebook) | ISBN 9781666339659 (hardcover) | ISBN 9781666339666 (paperback) | ISBN 9781666339673 (pdf) | ISBN 9781666339697 (Kindle edition)
Subjects: LCSH: California—Gold discoveries—Juvenile literature. | California—History—1846-1850—Juvenile literature.
Classification: LCC F865 .K48 2022 (print) | LCC F865 (ebook) | DDC 979.4/04—dc23/eng/20220629
LC record available at https://lccn.loc.gov/2022029326
LC ebook record available at https://lccn.loc.gov/2022029327

Editorial Credits
Editor: Carrie Sheely; Designer: Bobbie Nuytten; Media Researcher: Donna Metcalf; Production Specialist: Whitney Schaefer

Source Notes
Page 6, "I reached my hand . . . " "The Discovery of Gold," Library of Congress, https://www.loc.gov/collections/california-first-person-narratives/articles-and-essays/early-california-history/discovery-of-gold/#:~:text=I%20reached%20my%20hand%20down,and%20fields%20were%20soon%20deserted, Accessed March 2022

All internet sites appearing in back matter were available and accurate when this book was sent to press.

Table of Contents

Words in **bold** are in the glossary.

Introduction

In 1848, James Marshall discovered a nugget of gold while building a sawmill for John Sutter in California. Word quickly spread. Within months, thousands of people had left their jobs and families and flocked to California. They dreamed of striking it rich.

By the end of 1849, California's non-**Indigenous** population had risen by about 90,000 people. Between 1848 and 1852, $207 million worth of gold was collected.

THE CHANGING VALUE OF MONEY

The value of money, including the U.S. dollar, shrinks over time. This is due to **inflation**. It means what something was worth in the past is less than it is worth today. For example, a loaf of bread cost five cents in 1900. But it would cost more than 25 times that today. The $41 million worth of gold collected in 1850 would be worth $1.5 billion in today's dollars.

Sutter's Mill was built near the American River in California.

But how did the Gold Rush really pan out? How much gold was there? Was it easy to find? Did people become rich overnight? The Gold Rush had major impacts. But were all of them good? It's time to unpack this historical event and separate the facts from fiction.

 Fact!

The wave of newcomers began arriving in California in 1849. They were nicknamed "49ers."

Chapter One

Collecting Gold

Many stories about the Gold Rush make it seem like California was bursting with gold. But while there was a lot of gold, collecting it was another matter.

At first, it was possible to find gold lying on the ground. That's how James Marshall found his first piece of gold. "I reached my hand down and picked it up; it made my heart thump, for I was certain it was gold," he later recalled.

James Marshall

★ Fact!

For John Sutter, the Gold Rush was a disaster. He ended up losing his land and going bankrupt.

Miners panned for gold as the Gold Rush began.

But in most cases, collecting gold was hard, slow, backbreaking work. Many early gold miners used a method called panning. Miners would work 12-hour days washing pans in streams. This process separated the gold from dirt and gravel. After swirling the mixture around, the gold would sink to the bottom. The water, which came from snowmelt, was ice-cold. At the end of a day, miners often collected only a small amount of gold dust.

The easy pickings were quickly found. But then gold became more and more difficult to find, especially after 1850. Miners had to find new ways to collect gold. They also needed to dig deeper and move more dirt. The work became more dangerous.

In 1853, **hydraulic** mining became popular. High-pressure water hoses were aimed at the side of a hill. This process could bring down huge amounts of earth. The dirt was sent through long, narrow boxes to capture gold. It worked well for collecting gold. But entire hillsides were destroyed.

Hydraulic miners used the force of water to break apart rocky hillsides.

A DANGEROUS JOURNEY

Although they were already in the United States, getting to California was very difficult for those coming from the East Coast. There were three main routes. Some people sailed on a ship. They had to travel 17,000 miles (27,359) around the tip of South America. It could take six to seven months. A shortcut could be taken through the Isthmus of Panama. But travelers had to go through a dangerous jungle. Most people made the 2,000-mile- (3,219-km-) route over land, a trip of about seven months. But many died along the way from accidents, disease, and lack of food or water.

Shipping companies advertised to try to persuade people to travel to California in their ships.

Chapter Two

Striking it Rich?

Many stories about the Gold Rush are about people striking it rich. These stories make it seem like most people who came to California were successful.

It's true that many miners succeeded in the early days of the Gold Rush. They could earn in a few days what they used to make in a year. Some even collected so much gold that it was worth millions of dollars. But discoveries like these were very rare. There are only about 10 well-known examples of large gold strikes.

After only a few years, the chances of striking it rich became much lower. Miners began to work for mining companies rather than look for gold on their own. Instead of a new life of independence, miners ended up working for wages. It was not unlike the life they left back at home.

California miners pose with their equipment in the 1850s. Water flowed through the boxes, leaving any gold behind.

Even if someone got lucky, the money was quickly spent. Demand for goods was high and supply was low. This resulted in very steep prices. A single egg could cost about $25 in today's dollars. A pair of boots cost about $2,500 in today's dollars. Many people were worse off than before they came to California.

The high demand and prices meant riches for one group of people. These were the **merchants** who sold goods to the miners. Called "mining the miners," they sold food, clothes, and equipment and made a lot of money. One famous example was Levi Strauss. He made and sold strong pants from tent canvas that did not easily wear out.

WOMEN OF THE GOLD RUSH

Most of the Gold Rush miners were men. Only about 10 percent of the group were women. Upon arriving in California, women were in high demand for the household work they usually did at home. Women could get paid well for cooking, cleaning, sewing, and laundering miners' clothes. Some women opened businesses and ran newspapers, bookstores, shops, and boarding houses.

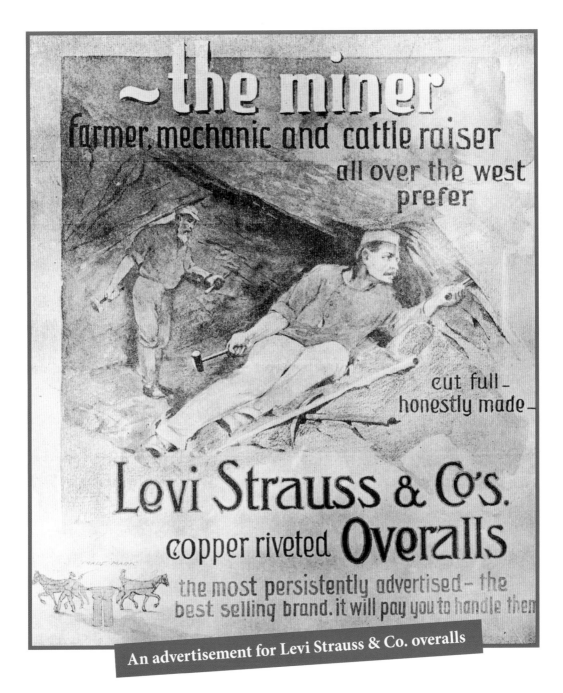

An advertisement for Levi Strauss & Co. overalls

Chapter Three

Paying the Biggest Price

While James Marshall is credited with finding the first gold, this wasn't true. Indigenous people living in California before the Gold Rush knew there was gold. But they didn't collect it because it didn't have any value to them.

But to others, gold meant riches. By 1854, 300,000 people had traveled to California in search of gold. It was the largest movement of people in U.S. history.

Most accounts of the Gold Rush focus on the large numbers of people who moved into the territory. Often left out is information about the terrible effect it had on those who were already living there.

Before the Gold Rush, about 160,000 Indigenous people and 700 to 1,000 non-Indigenous people were living in California. By the end of 1849, about 90,000 non-Indigenous people had arrived from across the U.S. and the world.

A California miner meets Indigenous people.
The flag attached to his rifle is a sign of peace.

The people coming from the eastern U.S. pushed Indigenous people off their land. Many were killed in the process. At first, companies hired many Indigenous people to work in the mines. But later, white miners began to view them as competition. Hostility toward Indigenous people grew, and they began to be attacked and killed.

By 1870, the number of Indigenous people in California had fallen by about 100,000. Great numbers died from diseases brought by non-Natives to the area.

White people pushed Indigenous people and miners from other countries away from areas where they wanted to look for gold.

Chapter Four

The Overlooked Immigrant Experience

Most of the stories about the Gold Rush focus on the Americans who traveled from the eastern parts of the country to California. But people from all over the world came in search of gold. Many of the first travelers to arrive came from Mexico, South America, and Asia. News of gold's discovery spread from ships stopping in California. In December 1848, U.S. President James Polk confirmed the discovery of gold. Afterward, Americans began to travel west to California.

The experience of **immigrants** has often been ignored in stories about the Gold Rush. Unfortunately, they were often hurt and treated unfairly.

As the number of people in California grew, the amount of gold shrank. Many American miners believed that California gold should belong only to whites. They began using threats and violence to drive foreign miners out of the land they had claimed for mining. In 1849, armed groups of white miners attacked several Chilean mining camps.

Chinese immigrants mine for gold in California using trays and pickaxes.

By 1852, about 25,000 Chinese people had arrived in California. They began working in mines that had been abandoned because most of the gold had been removed. While it was harder to collect, the Chinese workers were able to take out the gold that remained.

Anger soon became focused on the Chinese. White miners attacked Chinese miners to drive them away from their claims. In 1852, California passed a foreign miners tax of $3 per month in support of the anti-immigrant views.

Attacks on immigrants became more common as hostility grew toward them.

Driven out of the mines, many Chinese moved to San Francisco. There, they set up businesses and the first "Chinatown" in the United States. They opened restaurants as well as housekeeping and laundry services.

Chinese immigrants stand in front of a grocery store in Chinatown about 1885.

Fact!

Chinese immigrants later helped build the **transcontinental** railroad from 1863 to 1869. They laid about 700 miles (1,125 km) of tracks between California and Utah.

Chapter Five

A Landscape Forever Changed

The California Gold Rush brings to mind a picture of the lone miner panning for gold. But miners succeeding by working alone lasted only a short time. After just two years, mining required more equipment and people working together to reach buried gold. The new mining processes took a terrible toll on the landscape and **environment**.

The most harmful method was hydraulic mining. In 1853, Edward Mattison figured out how to blast hillsides with a high-pressure water hose. It could bring down an entire hillside in minutes. The mix of water and dirt would be directed into long stretches of wooden canals called **sluices**. Gold was collected from the mix.

Even early in the Gold Rush, miners looked for ways to make mining easier. Some used rocker boxes that helped sort out unwanted materials.

The resulting mix of water, dirt, and gravel flowed into the rivers and streams. Riverbeds and lakes became clogged. The bed of the Sacramento River was raised several feet after debris came down from the hillsides. When snow in the mountains melted, water flowed downstream, causing huge floods. Downstream farms and orchards were buried in mud and washed away. Cattle and wildlife drowned, and many people lost their homes. The towns of Marysville and Yuba City flooded often. In 1875, a major flood filled streets of Marysville with thick mud.

Farmers began to speak out against hydraulic mining. But the miners didn't want to stop the practice. It would put them out of work.

Over time, railroad companies also began to complain about hydraulic mining. It caused mud to spill onto the tracks. The practice was limited in 1884 after years of **protests** by farmers. But the California landscape was changed forever.

Hydraulic miners work near Dutch Flat, California, in 1868. The landscape nearby was greatly affected by the mining.

Chapter Six

Aftermath of the Gold Rush

The California Gold Rush was one of the most important events in the history of the United States. Many view it as a time of great adventure when fortunes were made.

But the truth of the Gold Rush is far less shiny. Few realized their dreams of wealth and a better life. Those who got richest were merchants. Most miners would have done just as well if they had stayed home working their old jobs.

Most miners worked very hard for little in return during the Gold Rush.

Much of the uglier side of the Gold Rush has been glossed over. The Indigenous people suffered greatly from it. Immigrants were treated poorly and attacked. Their gold was sometimes stolen from them. The environment was harmed.

One thing is certain—the Gold Rush sped up the movement of people to the American West. Today, California has one of the largest populations in the U.S. It all started with the lure of shiny bits of metal.

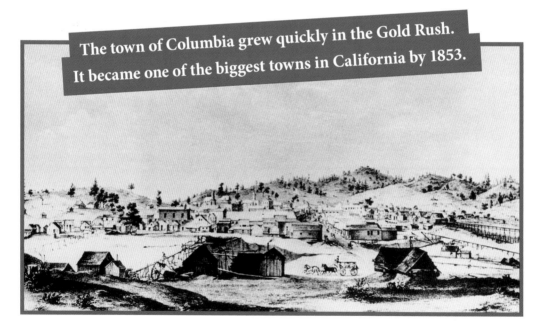

The town of Columbia grew quickly in the Gold Rush. It became one of the biggest towns in California by 1853.

Mythology of the Gold Rush

Fiction Gold was plentiful in California and easy to find.

Fact There was a lot of gold, but it was very hard to collect.

Fiction Many people struck it rich.

Fact There were a few miners who got rich. But merchants who sold goods and services to the miners were more likely to make a lot of money.

Fiction Miners were the people most affected by the Gold Rush.

Fact The Indigenous people who already lived in California were affected more than any group, and the impact on them was devastating.

Fiction Everyone had an equal shot at finding gold.

Fact Many immigrants were attacked and killed to drive them out of the gold fields.

Fiction The Gold Rush's main impact was on the population and economy of California.

Fact The environmental damage done by mining was serious and long-lasting.

Glossary

environment (in-VY-ruhn-muhnt)—the air, water, trees, and other natural surroundings

hydraulic (hye-DRAW-lik)—operated, moved, or brought about by using water

immigrant (IH-muh-gruhnt)—a person who leaves one country and settles in another

Indigenous (in-DIH-juh-nuhs)—a way to describe the first people who lived in a certain area

inflation (in-FLAY-shuhn)—an increase in prices

merchant (MUHR-chuhnt)—a buyer and seller of goods for profit

protest (PROH-test)—to object to something strongly and publicly

sluice (SLOOS)—a channel made by people through which water flows

transcontinental (transs-kon-tuh-NEN-tuhl)—crossing a continent

Read More

Caswell, Max. *My Life During the Gold Rush*. New York: Gareth Stevens Publishing, 2018.

Hyde, Natalie. *Gold Rushes*. New York: Crabtree Publishing Co., 2018.

Rusick, Jessica. *Joining the California Gold Rush: A This or That Debate*. North Mankato, MN: Capstone, 2020.

Wilkins, Veronica B. *California Gold Rush*. Minneapolis: Jump! Inc., 2020.

Internet Sites

Britannica Kids: California Gold Rush
kids.britannica.com/students/article/California-Gold-Rush/631740

Kiddle: California Gold Rush Facts for Kids
kids.kiddle.co/California_Gold_Rush

PBS LearningMedia: The Gold Rush
tpt.pbslearningmedia.org/resource/the-gold-rush-gallery/ken-burns-the-west/

Index

About the Author

Carol Kim is the author of several fiction and nonfiction books for kids. She enjoys researching and uncovering little-known facts and sharing what she learns with young readers. Carol lives in Austin, Texas, with her family. Learn more about her and her latest books at her website, CarolKimBooks.com.